Beat GST Notices with P.R.O.A.C.T. FRAMEWORK

REVEALING HIDDEN SECRETS EVERY BUSINESS OWNER MUST KNOW TO AVOID GST PENALTY

Beat GST Notices with P.R.O.A.C.T. FRAMEWORK

REVEALING HIDDEN SECRETS EVERY BUSINESS OWNER MUST KNOW TO AVOID GST PENALTY

CA. Shubham Agarwal
Partner | RSAG AND CO LLP
Chartered Accountant | | Faculty & Speaker

Available on amazonkindle
Worldwide Published by
Pendown Press
PREMIUM BUSINESS PUBLISHER

PENDOWN PRESS LLP

An ISO 9001 & ISO 14001 Certified Co.,

Regd. Office: 3767A, Kanhaiya Nagar,
Tri Nagar, Delhi-110035
Ph.: 8130886000, 9650072927
E-mail: info@pendownpress.com
Branch Office: 1A/2A, 20, Hari Sadan, Ansari Road,
Daryaganj, New Delhi-110002
Ph.: 011-45794768
Website: PendownPress.com

Edition: 2025
Price: ₹ 299
ISBN: 978-93-7217-938-5

Layout and Cover Designed by Pendown Graphics Team
Printed and Bound in India by Thomson Press India Ltd.

CONTENTS

DISCLAIMER

This book is written with the sincere intention of helping business owners better understand GST compliance, prevent common errors, and reduce the risk of litigation.

While every effort has been made to ensure the accuracy of the information shared, this book does not constitute professional or legal advice. GST laws, rules, and departmental practices are subject to frequent changes, and their interpretation may vary based on individual business circumstances.

Readers are advised to consult their own qualified tax advisor or consultant before making any decisions or taking actions based on the contents of this book. The author, contributors, and publisher shall not be held liable for any direct, indirect, or consequential loss arising from the use of the information provided.

Real-life stories and case studies included in this book have been adapted for learning purposes. Names and certain details have been changed to protect privacy.

By reading this book, you acknowledge and accept that the responsibility for applying the information lies solely with you.

DEDICATIONS & ACKNOWLEDGMENTS

This book is dedicated, first and foremost, to the people who have been the foundation of everything I am today.

To **my father, Mr. Mamraj Agarwal**, whose quiet strength, wisdom, and unwavering values have shaped my journey more than words can ever express.

To **my mother, Mrs. Rekha Agarwal**, whose love, patience, and prayers have always been my greatest source of courage.

To **my wife, Ridima**, who has stood by me through every late night, every moment of doubt, and every small victory, your faith in me has been my constant anchor.

And **to my little daughter, Akshvi**, who reminds me every day why the pursuit of meaningful work truly matters.

I owe deep gratitude **to all my teachers, gurus, and mentors**, each of whom has left an imprint on my thinking, guiding me not just with knowledge, but with perspective and purpose.

This book is also born out of the real challenges faced by the business community.

To all my clients and countless business owners, who are not just entrepreneurs but the true building blocks of our economy, thank you for trusting me with your struggles, your stories, and your aspirations. You have been both my inspiration and my teachers in this journey.

This book is not just my effort; it is a reflection of the love, guidance, and lessons I've received from all of you.

This book is as much yours as it is mine.

PREFACE

> ***"Avoiding GST notices isn't about luck or chance—it's about knowing what the department looks for before they do."***

Throughout my career, I have met hundreds of business owners. Many have come to me anxious, frustrated, or simply worn out, not because their businesses were failing, **but due to something even more overwhelming:**

- An unexpected GST notice
- A confusing penalty
- Or a compliance issue

All hidden deep in paperwork that no one had warned them about in time.

I have witnessed that sense of helplessness, the sleepless nights, the stress when a notice arrives, the continuous correspondence with officers, far too often. This experience led me to a clear decision: enough is enough.

This book is the outcome of that conviction.

Over the past decade, I have worked closely with business owners from diverse industries—

- Simplifying complex laws
- Guiding them through legal challenges
- Conducting departmental audits
- And helping them strengthen their compliance processes.

Through this, I have realized that **most GST issues do not arise suddenly; they build up gradually.**

However, with the right systems, mindset, and foresight, most can be avoided.

This book goes beyond GST laws and litigation tactics. It is about empowering business owners.

It aims to make compliance an advantage rather than a burden, focusing on prevention, confidence, and lasting relief.

Your Partner in Compliance & Litigation

CA. Shubham Agarwal

Partner | RSAG AND CO LLP

Chartered Accountant | | Faculty & Speaker

WHO AM I?

In the preface above, I have confidently staked claim to being your 'Compliance & Litigation Partner' and assured you that with this book, you will leverage compliance to thrive rather than it being a burden to be borne.

With a unique combination of expertise in finance, law, and technology, I am a dual-qualified Chartered Accountant and Law Graduate from the esteemed Faculty of Law at Delhi University.

For over a decade, I have guided business owners through the most challenging GST situations.

After obtaining my Chartered Accountancy in 2012, I worked at a leading CA firm in India, where I gained important experience in taxation and audit. Eager to deepen my legal understanding, I pursued an LLB from the Faculty of Law, University of Delhi.

When GST was introduced in July 2017, I recognized the law's complexity and the widespread lack of clear legal interpretation. Notices became frequent, and both the department and business owners struggled to navigate the new regime. This inspired me to focus on simplifying legal complexities and becoming a source of guidance in the GST ecosystem, benefiting both the department and business owners.

My professional journey began with Ernst & Young, but my mission soon grew to transform the GST experience for Indian businesses. Supported by credentials such as a GST certification from ICAI and a Diploma in Information Systems Audit (DISA), I offer more than consultancy—I am a trusted advisor for sustainable, risk-proof growth.

As a former Special Invitee to ICAI's National Indirect Tax Committee and an official GST Faculty Member, I have become a resource for both industry veterans and department officials. I have trained hundreds, spoken at prominent forums, and my insights have been featured nationally, including on the TV show *Good Evening India* and CBIC's official Twitter channels.

Whether analyzing anti-evasion strategies, managing high-stakes cases before the Directorate General of GST Intelligence (DGGI), or supporting clients through litigation, *I am driven by one principle: business owners deserve clarity, compliance, and control, not fear and fatigue.*

This book is more than a guide—**it's my mission to free business owners from GST anxiety.**

It is written by someone who has successfully helped hundreds do just that with a mission to provide relief, reliability, and results.

Here's a peek into what one of my clients has to say about our services.

Safeguarding Not Just Our Present But Our Future Too

We at One group, headquartered in Delhi, **with multiple locations all over India,** are engaged in the development of plots and the construction of affordable as well as luxury housing in many locations- currently 6 places in India. One of the fastest-growing Real Estate groups, we are the symbol of excellence and trust, shaping skylines across India. Celebrated for delivering skilfully designed projects, our debt-free model ensures stability and confidence in every endeavor.

We are delighted to share our experience working with CA. Shubham Agarwal (Partner) and CA. Ridima Goel (Partner) and their entire team of RSAG AND CO LLP for their exceptional Internal Audit services for our company. From the very beginning, they demonstrated a deep understanding of the complexities of the Real Estate sector and its regulations w.r.t to Internal audits.

Their audits were not just about identifying discrepancies but also providing actionable recommendations to strengthen our processes. Their ability to pinpoint potential risks and suggest corrective measures has been invaluable in safeguarding our business interests.

We highly recommend CA. Shubham Agarwal and his team to any real estate firm seeking reliable, detail-oriented, and strategic internal audit services.

Thank you, Shubham and team, for your exceptional work!

Best regards,

Udit Jain
Promoter
For ONE Group Developers

WHY THIS BOOK EXISTS? [AND WHY IT MIGHT JUST SAVE YOUR BUSINESS]

Have you ever experienced that sinking feeling when your accounts head walks in and says,

"Sir... GST notice aa gaya hai."

You freeze. Your mind races.

And one question echoes louder than the rest:

"But everything was being filed on time... so why this?"

You're not alone.

Across the country, business owners—people who work hard, run clean businesses, and trust their systems are suddenly finding themselves hit with GST notices, demands, and departmental scrutiny.

And most of the time, it's not because they've done something wrong.

It's because they didn't know what to check. Or what to prevent.

This book was born out of the frustration that business owners endure.

- The frustration of seeing smart entrepreneurs pay the price for someone else's mistake.
- Frustration of watching companies bleed money through penalties, interest, and blocked ITC.

- And the biggest frustration of all, realizing how easily most of this could have been avoided. Behind every notice is a signal that went unnoticed.
- Behind every penalty is a system that was missing.
- And behind every legal case is usually a missed chance to act early.

I've spent years working in the GST trenches.

With businesses, small and large.

Helping some sleep peacefully, and helping others come out of chaos.

In that journey, I found a pattern.

Certain mistakes kept showing up.

Certain loopholes kept catching people off guard.

And certain habits, once built, kept business owners safe even if a notice did come.

This book is here to share all of that with you.

It's not full of jargon. It's not a lecture.

It's a practical, honest guide to help you:

- Understand where the real risks lie
- Fix things before they become problems
- Build a GST system that protects your peace of mind
- And most importantly, feel in control again

You'll read true stories.

You'll learn how other business owners solved what you might be struggling with right now.

And you'll uncover six powerful secrets that very few professionals ever talk about.

This book was written to help you stop firefighting and start leading.

If GST has ever caused you anxiety, even a little bit, then I invite you to read on.

Because once you know what I'm about to share, you'll never look at GST the same way again.

"Over the years, I've listened to the fears, frustrations, and sleepless nights of hundreds of business owners. And what I've learned is this: most of these GST problems aren't inevitable, they're preventable.

My goal with this book is simple: to show you how to protect your business by using **lawful, strategic**, and **proactive** practices. You don't have to live in fear of the next notice. Let's build your GST defense **proactively**, not reactively. And most importantly, **legally**."

Here's what my clients have experienced, and you can experience this too, if you implement all that I share in this book.

From Pan India GST Chaos to Complete Clarity

CA Shubham Agarwal Became Our Single Window Solution

When our business expanded across almost 15 states, our GST troubles multiplied exponentially. Different jurisdictions, conflicting officer interpretations, and mounting compliance costs were choking our growth until we discovered Shubham's remarkable nationwide expertise.

The All-India GST Crisis We Faced

- Contradictory demands from multiple state authorities
- A huge amount was being spent annually on regional consultants
- Cases stuck in Telangana, Haryana, Karnataka, and Delhi simultaneously

Shubham was instrumental in solving our litigation issues with the following strategy—

- **One-Nation-One-Solution:** Handled all the cases across the six states with a centralized strategy.
- **Jurisdictional Mastery:** Leveraged local precedents from Kerala to help our Punjab case.
- **Virtual Resolution:** Settled the Karnataka case without physical hearings using tech-savvy representations.
- **Pan-India Professionals Network:** Shubham's all-India professional contact sphere helped in aligning with local consultants to conclude the cases with minimum physical visits.

Shubham ensures winning GST orders across India, quickly and affordably. He didn't just fix our past problems; he also protects us from future headaches.

For businesses working in multiple states, Shubham is more than an advisor; he is the 'Expert' who makes GST rules work in your favour.

Jagdish Moolchandani
Executive Director & CFO
Archies Ltd.
(Company Listed on the Indian Stock Exchange)

CHAPTER 1

THE GST ANXIETY EPIDEMIC

[HOW TO PROTECT YOUR BUSINESS FROM NOTICES AND PENALTIES]

A Business-Shattering Knock at the Door

It's 11:30 AM on a Wednesday. *Rakesh (Name changed), a second-generation business owner in Gurugram, is going about his day when his phone buzzes. A glance reveals a message from his accounts head. He expects something routine until he reads it:

"Sir, GST notice aa gaya hai. ₹28.5 lakh ka demand... plus penalty."

His heart sinks. He reads it again, trying to make sense of what's going on. His hands are suddenly cold.

How can this be happening?

Here's the kicker: Rakesh had been filing his returns on time. He trusted his Consultant to handle everything. So, how is it that this notice is accusing him of ineligible Input Tax Credit (ITC) for things that seem so... small?

- A supplier's GST number was cancelled retroactively three months ago
- A vendor's invoice wasn't showing up in GSTR-2B
- Credit had been claimed on services with the wrong HSN/SAC classification
- And there was no proof of payment to a few vendors within 180 days

Rakesh's mind races as he thinks,

- "How could I have caught all this?"
- "Isn't this why I hired a consultant?"
- "Now I'm paying the same tax again, plus penalties?"

In a moment, his entire cash flow is in jeopardy. His sleep is gone, and his trust in the system is shattered. And the truth is, this isn't an isolated incident.

It's happening to business owners everywhere, just like you.

The New Reality: GST Is No Longer Just a Filing Exercise

For years, I've heard business owners say:

"If we file on time and keep our invoices in order, we're good."

But here's the cold truth: That belief doesn't work anymore.

GST has evolved. It's no longer about filing returns and keeping your paperwork in order. The game has changed. **It's about matching, precision, and compliance intelligence.**

You might be unknowingly facing risks because of things you never thought twice about:

- Claiming ITC on things like canteen expenses, civil work, or blocked services
- Mismatches between your books and GSTR-2B
- Credit taken on invoices that aren't yet uploaded by the supplier
- Vendors whose GSTIN has been cancelled retroactively
- Not paying your suppliers within the 180-day window, which causes a credit reversal
- Incorrect HSN/SAC classifications are causing disputes over GST rates
- Reverse charge liabilities not reported or delayed

And here's the kicker: **The system is set up to catch all of this**. And it's catching it faster than ever.

So, What's Fueling the Surge in Notices?

1. **AI-Driven Scrutiny Is Now the Default** The GST Network (GSTN) is no longer just processing returns. It's **actively scanning** and **matching** data using AI. It checks your returns, supplier filings, e-way bills, and even your AIS and 26AS. A small mismatch? **Auto-flag → Auto-notice. One tiny error and the system flags you.**
2. **Departments Are Under Pressure to Show Results** Here's the reality for GST officers: They're judged by how many cases they raise, resolve, and recover. It creates a flood of notices, sometimes vague, often aggressive. And when you're on the receiving end of those notices, it can feel like you're under attack.
3. **Blind Spots in Traditional Consultant Services** Most Consultants handle GST filing mechanically; they file your returns and check the boxes. **But they miss the deeper details**:

- No **pre-audit checks**
- No **vendor compliance reviews**
- No **reconciliation alerts**

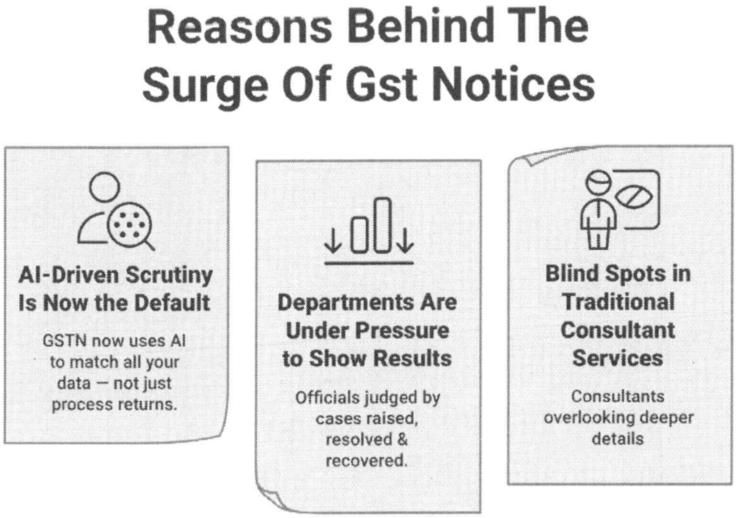

By the time a notice comes through, it's too late to fix things. The damage is done, and you're left scrambling to resolve a mess that could've been avoided with a little more vigilance.

"I Did Everything Right. Why Me?"

"I paid my taxes on time."

"I submitted my invoices."

"I didn't hide anything."

Yet, when the notice arrives, it feels like a personal attack. Business owners ask themselves: **"Why me?"**

Here's the thing:

In GST, **silence is not safety.**

Matching is.

You can't just file and forget. Every detail needs to be aligned because the system doesn't forgive mistakes, no matter how small.

The Real Emotions Behind the Balance Sheet

As someone who's been in this field for years, I can tell you what keeps business owners up at night isn't just the financial burden of a notice. **It's the emotional toll.**

I've seen it firsthand:

- The **harassment** of dealing with endless notices
- The **confusion** over the constantly changing rules
- The **helplessness** when vendors don't comply
- The **fear** of personal liability or even legal action

Some business owners have even stopped claiming ITC altogether. Others try to play it safe by under-claiming. But here's the reality: **both are poor choices**. It's like choosing between a **loss** and **living in constant fear**. And neither leads to sustainable growth.

It Doesn't Have to Be This Way

Look, this book isn't just another technical guide.

It's a **shield**.

A **strategy manual**.

A **peace-of-mind blueprint**.

Once you understand how the system really works and how to shift from **defense to offense,** you'll be in control. You'll learn how to:

- **Avoid costly mistakes** that can trigger scrutiny
- **Build a vendor ecosystem** that protects you, not punishes you

- Develop a **GST system** that's **audit-ready**, **litigation-proof**, and **stress-free**
- Reclaim your **time**, **cash flow**, and most importantly, your **peace of mind**

What's Coming Next

In the next chapter, I'll introduce you to **'The 6 Pillars of GST Prevention',** the same system I've used to help businesses like yours avoid the chaos of surprise GST notices and penalties.

Because **Prevention is not an expense,** it's your **business safety net**.

If you're tired of worrying about what's waiting for you in your inbox,

Turn the page. Relief starts now.

A Personal Note from the Author

"Over the years, I've listened to the fears, frustrations, and sleepless nights of hundreds of business owners. And what I've learned is this: most of these GST problems aren't inevitable, they're preventable.

My goal with this book is simple: to show you how to protect your business by using **lawful, strategic,** and **proactive** practices. You don't have to live in fear of the next notice. Let's build your GST defense **proactively,** not reactively. And most importantly, **legally."**

⃠⃠⃠⃠

CHAPTER 2

THE 6 PILLARS OF GST PREVENTION

[HOW SMART BUSINESSES STAY AHEAD WITH THE P.R.O.A.C.T. FRAMEWORK™]

Would you rather fight a fire or fireproof your house?

That's the choice every business owner unknowingly makes when it comes to GST.

Most people reach out after the notice.

But the smartest ones get help before the notice ever comes.

Over the years, I've handled hundreds of litigations and reconciliations. Through that experience, one truth has emerged clearly:

Prevention is not luck. It is a system.

That system is the PROACT Framework™.

Six practical, repeatable pillars that quietly protect your business while others remain exposed.

Let's explore each of them.

P: Pre-GST Audit and Assessment

Catch the cracks before the taxman does

What it is:

A monthly or quarterly internal review of your GST filings, ITC trail, return consistency, and documentation done before the department finds the gaps.

What it prevents:

- Undetected mismatches
- Repetitive reporting errors
- Use of ineligible credits
- Missed amendment windows

> **Monitoring Prevents Loss**
>
> One of our clients, Harshit*, **nearly missed a ₹6 lakh mismatch** between GSTR-1 and GSTR-3B in March. **We caught it just in time**. No notice. No penalty. Just peace of mind.
>
> *Real story (name changed)

R: Realtime Reconciliation System

GST doesn't wait. Why should your checks?

What it is:

Use tools or dashboards to match GSTR-2B with your books every month, not just at year-end.

What it prevents:

- Claiming credit for missing invoices
- Duplicate or skipped ITC
- Supplier-side mistakes you didn't cause but may still pay for

Common triggers caught:

- Invoice not in 2B
- Supplier GSTIN cancelled
- 180-day payment not made

Bonus Tip

Set alerts for high-value vendors.

If they default, you'll know before the department does.

O: Onboarding KYC and Vendor Vetting

Cheapest vendor today. Costliest mistake tomorrow?

What it is:

Before you finalise a vendor, check if they're compliant, not just cheap.

What it prevents:

- ITC denial from fake or fraudulent vendors
- Credit reversals due to retroactive GSTIN cancellations
- Notices under Rule 86A

Ask your vendors:

- Is GST registration active?
- Are returns up to date?
- Any past notices or litigation?
- Are they using the correct HSN?

Bonus Tip

Document all of it.

One saved screenshot can silence a notice.

A: Avoiding ITC Traps

Not all credits are created equal

What it is:

Train your team to recognise and avoid blocked or risky ITC claims before they happen.

What it prevents:

- Claims on blocked items like a car purchase or canteen bills
- Missed ITC on reverse charge
- Misclassification of services or assets

Practical step:

Create a simple visual chart of what's allowed, what's not, and what needs CA advice. Stick it near the desk of anyone booking purchases.

Bonus Tip

If you're not absolutely sure, pause. Ask. Then claim.

C: Configure Business Model for Tax Efficiency

Your structure can be your shield

What it is:

Structure your business to reduce tax burden legally, not just file returns.

What it prevents:

- Excess GST due to poor transaction planning
- Missed refunds, such as on exports or inverted duty
- Unnecessary RCM liabilities

Ideas to explore:

- Separate GST registrations where it helps
- Use warehousing strategically to optimise credit cycles
- Evaluate composition vs regular schemes, if eligible

> **Bonus Tip**
>
> The right structure today can save lakhs tomorrow.

T: Timely Compliance and SOP Culture

If GST lives in your culture, it won't show up in your notices

What it is:

Create an internal system where GST responsibilities are clearly defined, routinely followed, and never left to the last minute.

What it prevents:

- Late filings and unnecessary interest
- Missed amendment deadlines
- Errors due to confusion or lack of accountability

Build a simple SOP:

- Who checks what and when
- Clear roles for consultant, accountant, and business owner
- Escalation plan when something seems off

Bonus Tip

It's not about more work. It's about consistent clarity.

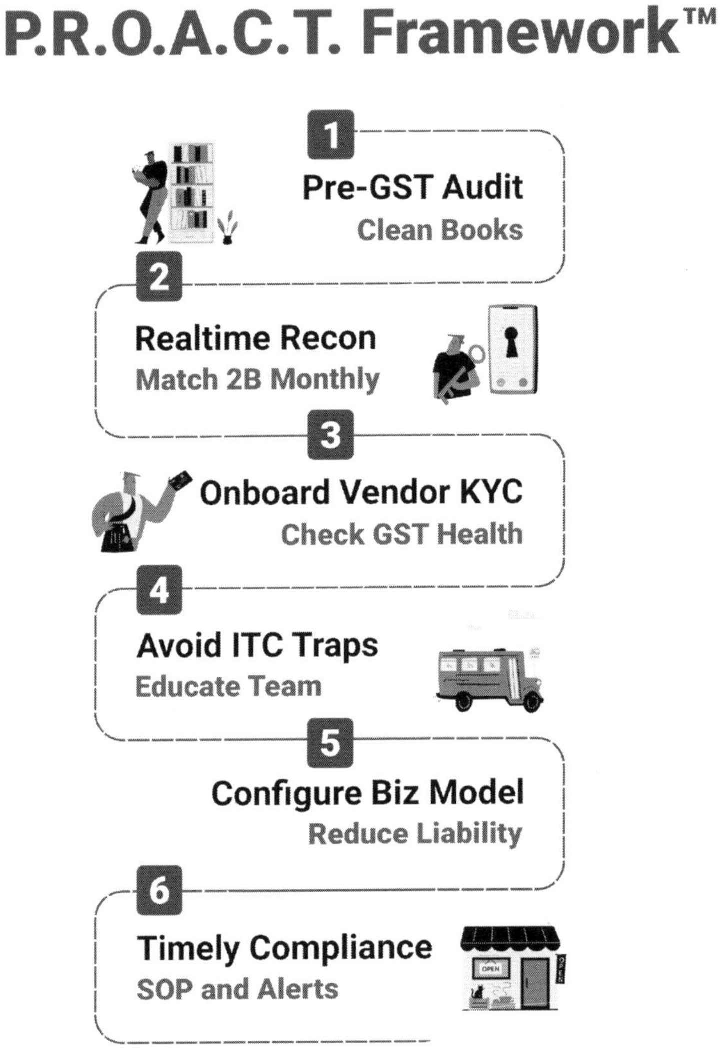

From Firefighting to Fortification

Most businesses spend their energy putting out fires.

But fireproofing is cheaper. And far more strategic.

When you adopt the P.R.O.A.C.T.

Framework™, here's what starts to shift:

- Your risk silently drops
- Your team gets trained and aligned
- Your business stays consistently protected

And perhaps most importantly —

You sleep better.

A Personal Note from the Author

Every time I've helped a client prevent a notice, I've seen their shoulders relax. That sigh of relief. That smile that says, "Thank God we did this early."

Prevention isn't just a technical strategy. It's a mindset. It's choosing peace over panic..

⦸⦸⦸⦸

CHAPTER 3

ITC: YOUR BIGGEST ASSET OR YOUR BIGGEST TRAP?

Input Credit Errors

Silently Killing Cash Flow and Inviting Notices

"We claimed what we were eligible for... so why are we in trouble?"

That was the first thing *Mehul (name changed) said when he walked into our office, visibly shaken.

Mehul was the **CFO of a mid-sized manufacturing company**. He had just **received a notice denying ₹36 lakhs worth of Input Tax Credit (ITC).**

The pain in his voice wasn't just about the numbers.

"All purchases were genuine. Invoices were with us. We've already used the credit... and now they want us to pay it all over again-with interest?"

We went to work.

A detailed review unearthed the following:

- Several invoices weren't appearing in GSTR-2B when the credit was claimed
- Credits had been taken on civil construction and canteen expenses
- One key vendor's GSTIN was suspended, and they never got an alert
- A few invoices had no payment trail within 180 days
- Some entries carried incorrect HSN codes, affecting eligibility

The result?

A storm of cash blockage, legal hustle, and weeks of emotional exhaustion.

The Illusion of Safety

On the surface, ITC feels like a reward. A way to lower your tax burden. And rightly so. It is one of the most powerful features of the GST regime.

But here's the twist: the very same ITC can backfire.

In fact, **mismanaged ITC is now *the most common trigger* for GST notices.** Not because businesses are dishonest, but because they're unaware.

What begins as a relief ends up damaging:

- Cash flow (credit reversed or blocked)
- Profitability (extra tax + 18% interest)
- Peace of mind (legal battles, SCNs, audit threats)

And the scariest part?

Most of these errors are completely unintentional.

The Invisible Traps Lurking in Your ITC Claims

Let's walk through the most common ITC pitfalls that silently damage businesses from within. Some may seem trivial, but they've cost businesses crores in litigation and penalties.

1. **Claimed Credit on Invoices Missing in GSTR-2B**

   You had the invoice. You booked it. You claimed the credit. But it wasn't in GSTR-2B that month.

   That one detail? Enough to deny your credit.

   What to do: Reconcile GSTR-2B every month. If it's not in 2B, it's not eligible, no matter how genuine your invoice is.

2. **Vendor's GSTIN Was Cancelled Retrospectively**

   The vendor was active when you bought the goods. But later, their GSTIN got cancelled with a backdated effect.

   Suddenly, your credit is at risk.

   What to do: Monitor vendor GSTIN status, especially your top suppliers. Tools exist for automated tracking. Use them. Use favourable case laws to your advantage.

3. **Blocked Credits Under Section 17(5): The Hidden Landmines**

   This section of the law is short in words but vast in consequences.

   Section 17(5) of the CGST Act defines a long list of scenarios where ITC is **not allowed,** even if the goods or services are genuinely used in business.

   Many businesses fall into this trap unknowingly, simply because the blocked categories don't always "look" ineligible at first glance.

Here's a practical and detailed list every business must understand, follow, and implement as part of its finance hygiene.

**(Caution: Read the exact language of the law along with the judicial pronouncements before availing or denying any Input tax credit. The following is only a simplified version of the section.)*

i. **Motor Vehicles and Conveyances**

   No ITC on motor vehicles with a seating capacity of 13 or fewer persons unless used for resale, transport of passengers, or driving training.

ii. **Vessels and Aircraft**

   ITC is not allowed unless used for resale, transport of goods/passengers, or flying instruction.

iii. **Services Related to Motor Vehicles, Vessels, Aircraft**

   Includes insurance, servicing, or repairs. These are blocked unless you're in that specific business or the asset itself qualifies under points 1 or 2 above.

iv. **Food and Beverages, Outdoor Catering**

   Blocked unless you are in the business of supplying the same goods or services.

v. **Beauty Treatment, Health Services, Cosmetic and Plastic Surgery**

   Blocked unless provided as part of a taxable outward supply.

vi. **Club Memberships, Health Club, and Gym Fees**

   ITC is not allowed even if provided to employees.

vii. **Employee Travel Benefits**

   Blocked unless such benefits are mandated under applicable labor laws.

viii. **Works Contract Services for Construction of Immovable Property**

If capitalised in books and not used for further works contract supply, ITC is blocked.

ix. **Construction of Immovable Property on Own Account**

Includes renovation, repairs, or alterations if capitalised. Plant & Machinery is an exception.

x. **Goods or Services Used for Personal Consumption**

Fully disallowed regardless of business context.

xi. **Goods Lost, Stolen, Destroyed, Written Off, or Given as Gifts or Free Samples**

Credit must be reversed in these scenarios.

xii. **CSR Expenditure (Corporate Social Responsibility)**

Courts have held that ITC is not available for goods/ services used to fulfil CSR obligations.

xiii. **Tax Paid Under Section 74**

ITC is disallowed for tax paid on the grounds of fraud, misstatement, or suppression of facts.

Some other credits which are blocked elsewhere in the law:

i. **Composition Dealer Purchases**

No ITC allowed on purchases made from composition scheme dealers.

ii. **Amount Written Back to Profit & Loss Account**

If vendor balances are written off or reversed, the corresponding ITC may need to be reversed.

iii. **Penalty and Delayed Payment Interest Received**

It can attract questions on whether ITC was correctly linked or overstated.

iv. **Rule 42 & 43 Violations**

Errors in proportionate credit reversal for inputs used in both taxable and exempt supplies can lead to ITC denial.

v. **POS Mismatches or Interstate Purchases Without Registration**

If the Place of Supply is outside the registered state and you don't have registration there, ITC becomes ineligible.

vi. **ITC Taken Without Receipt of Goods/Services**

ITC can only be claimed after actual receipt, not just on invoicing.

What to do: Build a Blocked Credit Compliance Layer. Train procurement and accounts. Put up physical posters in your finance department. Most importantly, treat this as a monthly audit item, not a year-end ritual.

4. **Credit Taken But Vendor Not Paid Within 180 Days**

If payment isn't made to the vendor within 180 days of the invoice date:

- The credit must be reversed
- Interest must be paid
- It can be reclaimed only after full payment

What to do: Build a system to auto-flag unpaid invoices nearing 180 days.

5. **Wrong HSN Code – Right Item, Wrong Classification**

You bought the right goods. But the invoice carried the wrong HSN.

Now, eligibility is disputed.

What to do: Ask vendors to match HSN codes with your purchase orders. Keep standardization at the procurement level itself.

6. **Claimed Credit After Expiry Date**

   Even if the credit is rightful, claiming it after the due date (30th Nov of the following financial year or filing of annual return, whichever is earlier) makes it void.

   What to do: Don't wait till year-end to reconcile. Run monthly ITC health checks.

What Most Businesses Get Wrong About ITC

Most litigation cases we've handled around ITC stem from three things:

- Lack of monthly reconciliation
- Poor communication between teams
- Blind trust in vendors without validation

ITC is your money, but sitting in the government's wallet.

To unlock it

- Your documentation must be clean
- Your vendors must be compliant
- Your systems must be sharp

This isn't about being perfect. It's about being prepared.

The 6-Step ITC Clean-up Blueprint

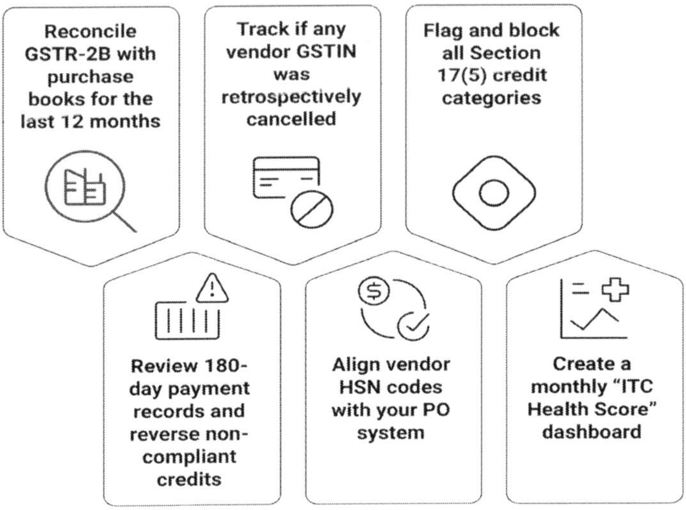

A Quiet Victory: ₹21 Lakhs Saved Without a Fight

A client once came to us with ₹21 lakhs of ITC under threat due to GSTR-2B mismatches and vendor issues.

We didn't panic. We acted.

- Vendors were contacted.
- Four corrected their returns
- Two appealed against their cancellation and got reinstated
- All reversals were corrected in the books with full documentation

When the department came for an audit, everything was in place.

No demand. No penalties. Just relief.

That's the power of pre-emptive clean-up.

A Note from Me to You

ITC is not just a compliance item. It's your working capital. It's your cash flow lifeline.

And it's also your risk—if left unmanaged.

In today's environment, it's no longer enough to claim credit. You must *defend* it, document it, and *earn* it.

As someone who's spent years in the trenches of GST litigation, I say this with full responsibility:

Most GST pain can be avoided—not by being reactive, but by being system-driven.

Let's shift from asking "Why did this happen?" to "How can we make sure it never happens again?"

Because when ITC is managed right, it doesn't just reduce tax. It protects your peace of mind.

⦸⦸⦸⦸

CHAPTER 4

WHEN THE VENDOR BECOMES THE VILLAIN!

How to Protect Your Business from Other People's GST Mistakes

*Siddharth (name changed) ran **a successful trading company in Delhi.** His internal team was sharp. Invoices were tallied, returns filed on time, and payments released with discipline.

Everything looked perfect—until the morning they received a GST notice.

- "Input Tax Credit of ₹11,04,000 disallowed.
- **Reason:** The Supplier did not file GSTR-1. GSTIN cancelled retrospectively."

Siddharth was stunned.

"But I bought genuine goods. I paid the full tax. I have every invoice and proof. How can this be happening?"

Unfortunately, that's exactly how it happens.

Under the GST law, particularly Section 16(2)(c), your Input Tax Credit is valid *only if your supplier pays tax to the government*.

It doesn't matter if you've done your part.

If your vendor fails, the system punishes you.

And just like that, Siddharth's business took a hit—not because of something he did wrong, but because of what his vendor failed to do.

The Hidden Reality: GST Isn't a Solo Game

GST was designed as a unified tax ecosystem. That means your compliance is directly tied to the compliance of every vendor you deal with.

You can:

- Purchase genuine goods
- Pay full GST to the supplier
- Maintain every invoice properly

But if your vendor:

- Doesn't upload your invoice in GSTR-1
- Has their GSTIN cancelled (even retroactively)
- Or simply doesn't pay the tax they collected from you...

Then the credit you claimed is denied!

It's like you're driving a clean car, but you get fined because the bridge you crossed wasn't built properly.

The Most Common Vendor Pitfalls That Hurt You

Let's look at some of the ways in which a vendor's mistakes become your liability:

1. **GSTR-1 Not Filed**

   If the vendor doesn't report your invoice in their GSTR-1, it doesn't show up in your GSTR-2B. And without that reflection, your credit is denied—simple as that.

2. **Cancelled GSTIN**

   Sometimes, GST registrations are cancelled by the department retroactively. You may not even know about it. But if your invoice falls in the period when their GSTIN was technically inactive, your ITC can be disallowed.

3. **Vendor Doesn't Pay Tax**

   Even if the invoice shows up in GSTR-2B, the department has the right to deny your credit if the vendor doesn't deposit the tax with the government. That's the hard sting of Section 16(2)(c).

4. **Fake or Dubious Invoices**

   Some vendors issue invoices without actual supply, especially in high-margin sectors. If the department flags that vendor as fraudulent, even genuine buyers like you can get trapped in the fallout.

5. **Incorrect Classification or Tax Rate**

   Even a technical error like misclassifying the HSN or applying the wrong tax rate can come back to haunt you. If the department later challenges the classification, they'll claw back the credit with interest and a penalty.

Your Best Defense: Build a Vendor Risk Framework (VRF)

If vendors can break your compliance, it only makes sense to treat them as part of your internal controls. A Vendor Risk Framework helps you screen, monitor, and safeguard your ITC.

Here's how to build one:

Step 1: Basic KYC Before Onboarding

Before working with any vendor, ask for:

- Their PAN and GST registration certificate
- Proof of business (a website, shop photo, or premises address)
- A quick check of their GSTR-1 and 3B filing history
- Any red flags—like pending legal cases or past cancellations

Step 2: Monthly Vendor Health Scorecard

Track each vendor's health based on these criteria:

- Are they filing GSTR-1 and 3B regularly?
- Are their invoices showing up in your GSTR-2B?
- Is their GSTIN still active?
- Have they been flagged or cancelled recently?

Score them monthly:

- Full score? **Green.**
- Minor lapses? **Yellow—monitor closely.**
- Serious issues? **Red—pause or withhold ITC until resolved.**

Step 3: Tighten Your Purchase Terms

Your purchase orders or contracts should clearly mention:

"GST ITC shall be paid only if the invoice appears in GSTR-2B and the vendor remains GST-compliant."

This language can act as a commercial and legal deterrent.

Step 4: Automate and Monitor

For growing businesses, manual tracking isn't scalable. Use GST compliance software or reconciliation tools that alert you automatically if:

- A vendor's filing lapses
- Their GSTIN is suspended
- Invoices are missing from your 2B

Build a Vendor Risk Framework (VRF)

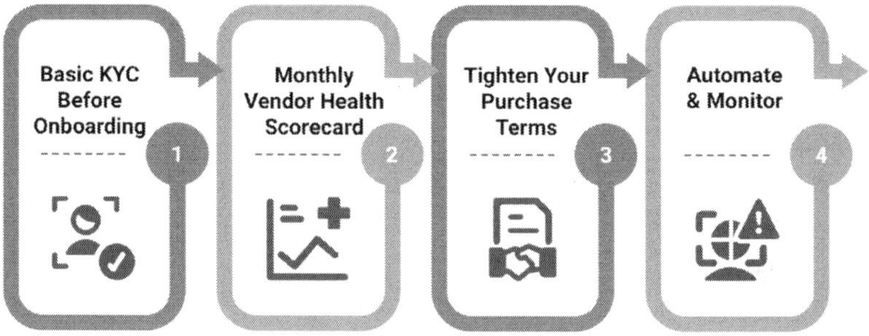

An Exporter Avoids a ₹18 Lakh Disaster

A Case Study

One of our exporter clients was about to **claim input credit worth over ₹18 lakhs when we flagged two of their key vendors.**

Both had their GSTINs suspended.

Before taking credit, the client:

- Checked the GST portal alerts
- Reached out to vendors to correct their filings
- Withheld payments until compliance was restored

The Outcome?

- No notice.
- Full credit preserved.
- ₹18 lakhs saved.
- And the peace of mind that comes from doing it right.

A Personal Note

In GST, your vendor isn't just someone you buy from. They're a link in your tax chain. If they break, your entire system feels the shock. The rules may feel harsh, but they're real. And the only way to protect your business is to be vigilant, proactive, and precise.

You've worked too hard to grow your business. Don't let someone else's mistake become your penalty.

Surround yourself with responsible vendors. Build systems that protect your cash flow. And remember, compliance is a team sport. Make sure you choose your team wisely.

⦸⦸⦸⦸

CHAPTER 5

Red Flags That Invite GST Notices

The Hidden Patterns That Most Businesses Overlook

"Most GST notices don't come out of the blue.

The signs were always there, buried in:

- Your returns
- Your vendor's behavior,
- Or your trial balance.

The real problem? No one showed you how to read them."

This chapter gives you a powerful tool—**a Basic GST Radar.**

It's not fancy. It's not technical. But if you check this every month, you'll spot the cracks before they turn into penalties.

I call it the Red Flag Checklist.

The Red Flag Checklist

20 Triggers That Need Your Monthly Attention

These are the signals that GST officers often use as starting points. If you're seeing even 3 or 4 of these in your business, you're not in the green zone anymore.

1. **ITC Claimed More Than Available in GSTR-2B**

   If you're claiming more input credit than what's reflected in 2B, expect ASMT-10 or reversal notices sooner or later.

2. **Mismatch Between GSTR-1 and 3B**

   If you're declaring turnover in GSTR-1 but not paying the corresponding tax in 3B, the system flags this as under-reporting.

3. **Supplier Didn't File GSTR-3B**

   Even if the invoice is uploaded in GSTR-1, if your supplier hasn't filed 3B or paid the tax, your credit is at risk under Section 16(2)(c).

4. **Difference Between GSTR-2A and 3B**

   Sometimes old-school 2A vs 3B mismatch is used to initiate audits. Don't ignore it.

5. **Dealing with Cancelled Suppliers**

   If the supplier's registration is cancelled—especially *retrospectively*—ITC can be denied completely.

6. **RCM Supply Mistagged by Supplier**

   The supplier wrongly marks their invoice as RCM. You ignore it. The department sees a mismatch. You get the notice.

7. **Place of Supply Doesn't Match Your State**

   POS showing another state? IGST credit will be disallowed. Happens often in inter-branch or logistics supplies.

8. **Payment Not Made Within 180 Days**

   Under Rule 37, you must reverse ITC with interest if the supplier is not paid within 180 days. Many forget this small clause.

9. **Interest Due on the Delayed Cash Portion of GSTR-3B**

   Even a short delay in paying tax in cash triggers auto-interest at 18%. Portal doesn't forget.

10. **Late Fees Piling Up**

    Late filing of GSTR-1, 3B, or 9 quietly builds late fees. System-generated notices now chase these regularly.

11. **Wrong Application of Rule 42 & 43**

    If you use common inputs for exempt and taxable supplies, but don't apportion properly, a reversal is required.

12. **Claiming Blocked Credits (Section 17(5))**

    Credits on canteen, construction, motor vehicles, etc., are not allowed. Still claimed? Expect full reversal + interest.

13. **Miscellaneous Income Not Reported**

    Incentives received, advances forfeited, provisions written back—these must be declared in GSTR-1. Missing this can trigger undervaluation notices.

14. **Creditors or Liabilities Written Back Without GST Reversal**

    If a vendor payable is written off in the books, any ITC taken earlier might need reversal.

15. **Interest or Penalty Received From Customers**

    Late payment charges from clients are taxable under GST. Often ignored. But departments don't miss it.

16. **Scrap Sale Not Declared**

    The sale of scrap, waste, or by-products without charging GST is a common mistake. It falls under taxable supply.

17. Export or Advance Not Realised

If export proceeds or advance receipts are not received in time, the refund gets reversed or the ITC is clawed back.

18. Wrong HSN or GST Rate Used

An innocent-looking HSN error can change everything—wrong rate, wrong tax, wrong credit.

19. Claiming Exemption Without Fulfilling Conditions

If you're using an exemption, make sure all conditions under the notification are met. Otherwise, the full tax becomes payable.

20. Mismatch in Turnover: Trial Balance vs GSTR-1/9 vs Books

Your GST returns must match your books. Many notices now come from financial audit mismatches.

What You Can Do Today

- Print this checklist.
- Share it with your team.
- Review it every month.
- You don't have to fix all 20 in one shot.
- But even if 3–4 of these are red, take them seriously.

GST notices don't strike like lightning.

They build up slowly, like a brewing storm.

Learn to read the clouds, and you'll never get caught in the rain.

⦸⦸⦸⦸

CHAPTER 6

DECODING GST NOTICES

[HOW TO SPOT RED FLAGS, UNDERSTAND THE LANGUAGE, AND RESPOND SMARTLY]

Caught Unaware & No One To Take Responsibility

"Why did I get this? What do they even want?"

That's exactly what *Rajeev (name changed), the owner of a mid-sized packaging company in Noida, muttered as he stared at the screen. A new message had popped up on the GST portal.

Notice: ASMT-10

Reason: ***Discrepancy in ITC claimed vis-à-vis GSTR-2B. Justify variance within 15 days or face reversal with interest.***

Rajeev was stunned. He thought everything was in order.

He immediately called his accountant.

His accountant shrugged.

Now Rajeev had 10 working days to reply to a document full of jargon and legal references he didn't fully understand.

This is where most business owners slip—

They either **panic and overreact...** or **ignore and delay**.

Both are expensive mistakes.

What Is a GST Notice, Really?

Let's demystify it.

A GST notice is not a penalty. It's not a punishment.

It's more like the department raising its hand and saying,

"We noticed something. Can you explain?"

It could be:

- A routine clarification
- A nudge before action
- Or a serious lead-up to an audit or litigation

The notice itself is **not the problem**.

How you respond is what determines the outcome.

Types of GST Notices You Might Receive

Not all notices are created equal. Some are soft taps, others are loud knocks. Here's a simple table to decode the most common ones:

Notice Type	What It Means	Common Triggers
GSTR-3A	Reminder for not filing returns	Missed or late return filing

ASMT-10	Discrepancy in your claimed returns	ITC is more than GSTR-2B, mismatch in turnover etc
RFD-08	Refund rejection	Incomplete documentation or wrong claim etc
SCN (Show Cause Notice) u/s 73 or 74 or 74A	Explain why action shouldn't be taken	Based on audits, investigations, and red flags
DRC-01	Summary of demand	The officer concludes you owe tax
DRC-07	Final demand	Pay tax, interest, and penalty or file an appeal

When A Notice Arrives

What Should You Do When a Notice Arrives?

Step 1: Stay Calm, But Don't Wait

Every notice comes with a clock. **Reply timelines matter.** Miss them, and you lose your say.

Step 2: Investigate the Real Issue

Check your:

- GSTR-1, GSTR-3B, and GSTR-2B
- Vendor filings and ledgers
- Books of accounts and reconciliation logs

Is it a genuine liability? Or just a mismatch in timing or format?

Step 3: Draft a Professional, Point-wise Reply Include:

- Clear explanation of each point
- Relevant GST rules or circulars
- Reconciliation sheets, invoices, and portal extracts
- Keep your tone factual, respectful, and logical

Avoid sounding defensive. Avoid blaming. Be precise.

Step 4: Seek Representation If Needed

If the notice escalates to SCN or DRC-01, it's time to bring in a professional.

Don't go solo in a hearing unless you're fully prepared.

Example:

A ₹3.24 Lakh ITC Mismatch

The Notice Says: *"Mismatch of ITC claimed in 3B vs 2B for May 2024: ₹3,24,000"*

What You Can Reply:

- Present a side-by-side table comparing GSTR-2B and your purchase register
- Highlight that the vendor filed the invoice late
- Attach updated 2B and vendor communication
- Clarify that there is **no loss to the revenue**, only a timing mismatch
- Include a signed self-declaration

A Personal Word of Advice

A GST notice is **not the end of the road**—

It's an invitation to step up, respond smartly, and prove your case.

Over the years, I've seen many clients turn things around—just by responding the right way.

It's not about knowing every section.

It's about being alert, calm, and clear-headed when it matters most.

And the best part?

When you learn to decode these notices once, they'll never scare you

⊘⊘⊘⊘

CHAPTER 7

THE LITIGATION PROOF LAYER

Building a GST Defense So Strong

You Don't Fear the Department

"Even if a notice comes, I'm not worried anymore."

That's what *Ankit (name changed), a business owner in the manufacturing space, told us after a six-month transformation in his GST practices.

He wasn't spared from notices.

One questioned a minor GSTR-2B mismatch.

Another came from the anti-evasion wing about ITC on transport vendors.

But neither led to any demand.

No penalty. No prolonged follow-up. No late-night stress.

Why?

Because everything — invoices, reconciliations, payment proofs — was already in place.

Before the officer asked.

He said,

"The notice felt like a formality... not a threat."

That's the mindset this chapter is here to build.

Why You Still Need a Defense — Even If You're Doing Everything Right

Let's be honest.

Even the most compliant businesses can get a GST notice.

Some are automated. Some are officer-driven. Some arise from vendor faults.

But when your **internal defense is strong**:

- ➢ Your records are clean and complete
- ➢ Your GST position is backed by logic and documentation
- ➢ Your responses are swift and confident
- ➢ Your team knows how to handle pressure

You don't panic.

You prepare, respond, and move on.

That's what being litigation-proof means.

The 6 Layers of Litigation -Ready GST Defense

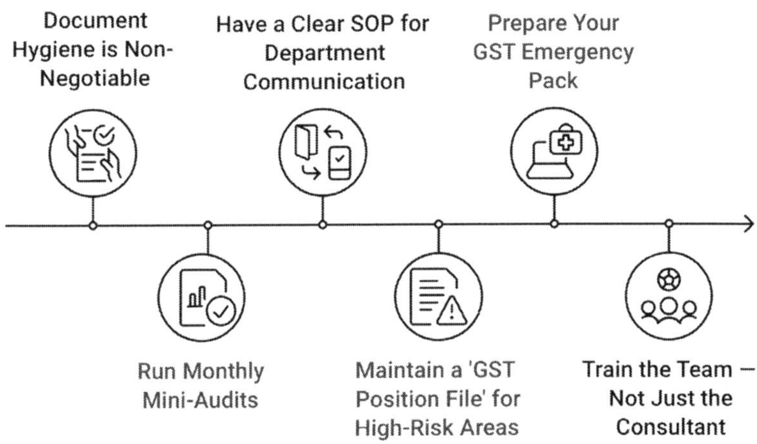

The 6 Layers of Litigation-Ready GST Defense

1. Document Hygiene is Non-Negotiable

The first line of defense is paperwork that's clear, complete, and current.

Keep ready:

- Tax invoices with full details
- E-way bills and delivery proofs
- Vendor agreements and POs
- Payment trails within 180 days
- Matched ledgers (books vs returns)

Bonus Tip

Build a "GST Compliance Folder" (digital or physical) — organised vendor-wise and month-wise. You'll thank yourself later.

2. Run Monthly Mini-Audits

Don't wait for a statutory auditor or a surprise departmental visit.

Every month, review:

- GSTR-2B vs purchase register
- GSTR-1 vs 3B turnover
- High-value supply mismatches
- Supplier GSTIN status
- Use of blocked or ineligible credits

Bonus Tip

Set a 30-minute GST review call with your consultant or finance head every month. Treat it like brushing your teeth — preventive and essential.

3. **Have a Clear SOP for Department Communication**

   If a notice lands or a query comes in:

   - Acknowledge within 24 hours
   - Route all replies through a single authority (your consultant or authorised signatory)
   - Keep tone respectful and fact-based
   - Maintain a dedicated email trail

Bonus Tip

Create a shared email like **gst@yourcompany.com** — accessible to your consultant, finance head, and one director. Clarity avoids chaos.

4. **Maintain a 'GST Position File' for High-Risk Areas**

   Some areas are grey, like HSN classification, RCM, or treatment of bundled supplies.

   Don't just take a stand. **Document the why**.

   Include:

   - Legal interpretation
   - Relevant circulars or advance rulings
   - Internal discussions or board memos
   - The logic behind the treatment you followed

Bonus Tip

If a demand ever arises, this file proves your intent was genuine — and that matters.

5. **Prepare Your GST Emergency Pack**

   What if an officer walks in today?

   Keep this ready and updated every quarter:

   - GSTR-1, 3B, 2B, 9, 9C for the last 2 years
   - Vendor-wise ITC register
   - Payment proofs for major purchases
   - ITC trend charts
   - Contact sheet: consultant, internal SPOC, legal counsel

Bonus Tip

This is your **GST First-Aid Box**. Pack it. Label it. Update it.

6. **Train the Team — Not Just the Consultant**

   One wrong entry by your accounts assistant can undo months of clean compliance.

   Train your internal team on:

   - Eligible vs blocked credits
   - Validating vendor health
   - GST-sensitive transactions (scrap, barter, CSR)
   - Filing deadlines and interest triggers

Bonus Tip

A GST-compliant company isn't made by one expert. It's a team sport. Everyone plays a role.

A Case Snapshot:

From ₹29 Lakh Threat to Zero Demand

A logistics company client was selected for audit.

Preliminary findings showed potential ITC reversal of ₹ 29 lakh due to:

- Cancelled vendor GSTINs
- Missing documents
- Confusion over RCM entries

But their groundwork was solid:

- All reconciliations were already in place
- Bank trails, invoices, and POs matched
- They had a GST position file, an internal SOP, and a documented process

The audit was closed in just 3 meetings.

No further questions. No demand. No litigation.

A Note from Me to You

"Litigation-proofing isn't about perfection. It's about preparation. It's the confidence that comes from knowing - if someone knocks, you're ready."

Build your GST system in a way that doesn't just prevent notices...

...but gives you peace even when one arrives.

That's not just compliance. That's power.

⃠⃠⃠⃠

CHAPTER 8

When Structure Saves You

Is Your Business Model Leaking GST or Saving Lakhs?

"Compliance wasn't my problem. Structure was."

That's what *Deepak (name changed) realized after running his **trading business across four states for five years.**

He had everything in place—returns filed on time, vendors verified, and reconciliations done monthly.

Still, he was paying 8–10% more in GST compared to peers in the same industry.

It didn't make sense at first.

Until we took a closer look.

His business model was clean... but inefficient from a GST lens.

Here's what we found:

- Goods were being routed through states that added an unnecessary tax layer.
- Office rent invoices from other states couldn't be used for ITC.
- Contracts with vendors shifted the reverse charge liability to him, unintentionally.
- And he was using just one GSTIN, despite having operations in four different states.

A few structural changes–nothing aggressive or grey–just intelligent alignment with the law–and he:

- Saved ₹14 lakhs annually in tax
- Cleared all refund bottlenecks
- Didn't receive a single notice in the next 18 months

That's what this chapter is about: **How smart structuring can become your GST advantage.**

Why Structure > Filing

GST isn't just about returns or reconciliations. It's about **how your business is built**.

Your:

- Entity and ownership structure
- State-wise registration strategy
- Billing and invoicing patterns
- Vendor and contract design
- Use of assets across states

...all directly affect your GST burden, ITC eligibility, refund delays, and risk of notices.

The hard truth?

Even the most punctual filer can bleed money if the business model itself is flawed.

The Hidden Structural Traps That Drain Your GST

Let's decode the most common structural issues that quietly add cost and attract scrutiny:

1. **One GSTIN Across Many States:** If you're operating in multiple states but using a single GST registration:
   - You end up doing interstate billing to yourself.
   - Lose ITC on local office expenses (like rent, electricity).
   - Appear non-compliant in state-level audits.
   - It can be a violation of Section 22 of the CGST Act 2017.

   What to do:

   Take a GSTIN in every state where you have a physical presence, offices, warehouses, or billing points. It gives you cleaner books and local ITC.

2. **Misaligned ITC Flow Between Entities:** Often in group businesses, one company pays, but another uses the credit. That's a red flag.

   What to do: Ensure that the entity availing ITC is the same one where the goods/services are consumed and billed.

3. **Poorly Worded Contracts Trigger RCM:** Services like manpower, legal, freight, etc., can silently shift the reverse charge to you if not structured well.

   What to do: Draft contracts that clearly assign tax liability to the supplier, if legally possible.

4. **Renting in Personal Name:** Offices or godowns rented in the director's name (instead of the business name) block your ITC and create RCM confusion.

   What to do: Ensure rent agreements are between the registered landlord and the GST-registered entity with proper invoicing.

5. **Bundled Supplies = Tax Rate Confusion:** When goods and services are combined without clarity, the wrong tax rates are applied. This can trigger 5% vs 18% disputes.

What to do: Break components clearly. Or seek an advance ruling when in doubt.

6. **Faulty Export/SEZ Structure:** Refunds often get stuck due to missing LUTs, using blocked credits, or delayed filing.

   What to do: File LUTs timely, avoid ineligible ITC in the refund pool, and align your export documentation carefully.

7. **Paying Unnecessary IGST on Imports:** Importing services like design, tech, or consulting? Sometimes, your model may create RCM even when it's avoidable.

   What to do: Re-draft contracts and supply chains to separate offshore services from Indian taxable events, where legally viable.

Smart Structuring = Strategic Edge

Now, let's talk about how you can flip the script:

1. **Get GSTINs Wherever You Work**

   It's not a burden—it's a tool. Local registration gives you:

   - Input credits on state-level costs
   - Better audit optics
   - Quicker refund cycles

2. **Align Warehouses with Billing**

   If your goods move from State A but you bill from State B, double tax could apply. Always match the billing point with the movement.

3. **Outsource with Strategy, Not Habit**

   Don't just pick vendors based on price. Choose those who:

   - Are GST compliant
   - Accept tax liability where it makes sense
   - Issue correct invoices on time

4. **Design Contracts Like a Consultant Would**

   Each contract should clearly define:

   - Who bears the tax
   - What HSN/SAC applies
   - What happens if the department raises a demand
   - Invoice timelines and formats

A Case Snapshot: From Struggle to Structure

A mid-sized SaaS company had:

- Offices in 3 states, but only 1 GSTIN
- Rent ITC losses in two locations
- Repeated notices on the place of supply for online services

After a structural audit:

- They took state-wise registrations
- Segmented vendor contracts
- Aligned exports under LUT

The Result?

- ₹11 lakh in tax savings
- 2 notices dropped
- No audit friction in the next return cycle

A Final Word from the Author's Desk

"Most business owners think GST is about returns. It's not. It's about how your operations speak the language of tax."

When your structure is clean, your tax liability shrinks, your refunds flow, and your risk drops.

The goal isn't just to avoid notices—it's to build a business that the department has no reason to doubt.

CHAPTER 9

WHAT YOUR CONSULTANT MAY NOT TELL YOU

Bridging the GST Advisory Gap Costing You Peace, Protection, and Profit

"We filed everything... Still got a notice."

This is one of the most common things I hear from business owners, and it always begins the same way: confusion, then frustration.

*Neha (name changed), **who runs a successful chain of electronics stores**, called in panic one afternoon. She had just received a **show cause notice: ₹18.7 lakhs worth of ITC mismatch flagged.** She was stunned.

"But everything's filed on time," she said. "GSTR-1, 3B, even the annual return."

She called her consultant.

"Aapne toh filing ki thi na?"

"Yes, ma'am, sab file ho gaya tha."

And technically, he wasn't wrong. Filing *was* done.

- But reconciliation hadn't been.
- Vendor statuses weren't being tracked.
- ITC wasn't being reviewed. No red flags were raised.

No preventive advisory was given.

That's when Neha realised the hard truth:

Compliance is not the same as strategy.

The Core Problem: Filing ≠ Advisory

Most traditional consultants are excellent at paperwork.

They:

- File returns
- Upload invoices
- Handle basics when pushed
- Respond *after* the problem comes

But here's what they often don't do:

- Flag high-risk ITC entries before they turn into notices
- Track supplier defaults, defaulters, or GSTIN cancellations
- Guide you on how to structure transactions to reduce GST liability
- Conduct internal audits or preventive reviews
- Train your in-house accounts team
- Build a defense file even when there's no active litigation

This gap between filing and true advisory is where peace of mind is lost, where profits leak, and where preventable notices arise.

Where Businesses Expect Support — But Don't Get It

Let's break it down to where most owners are left exposed without even knowing it.

1. **Vendor-Related ITC Risk**
   - No monthly GSTR-2B vs books checks
   - No alerts when a vendor stops filing or their GSTIN gets cancelled
   - No vendor grading system or compliance-based onboarding
2. **Blocked Credit Advisory (Section 17(5))**
   - Credit wrongly taken on the canteen, CSR, gifts, and construction
   - Most consultants don't highlight these unless asked directly
3. **Contract Structuring for GST-Efficient Transactions**
   - No help in drafting contracts that avoid reverse charge or mismatched HSNs
   - No strategy to reduce output tax by revisiting supply chains
4. **Prevention vs Response**
   - They respond after the notice
   - Rarely do they build systems that help avoid notices altogether
5. **Financial Data vs GST Return Reconciliation**
   - No linkage between your trial balance and what's filed in GSTR-1, 3B, or 9
   - This gap becomes a landmine during audits and scrutiny

6. Missed Refunds or Credit Opportunities

- Exporters lose lakhs in unclaimed refunds
- Inverted duty businesses often get stuck due to procedural delays

What This Costs You

Let's be direct. The advisory gap can cost you:

- ➢ Lakhs in disallowed ITC
- ➢ Lakhs more in penalties and interest
- ➢ Late fees, stress, and sleepless nights
- ➢ Time spent managing notices instead of running your business
- ➢ Loss of confidence in your own systems — and in the ecosystem itself

So, What's the Solution?

You don't need to fire your existing consultant. But you *do* need to build a stronger GST defense system, one that's proactive, strategic, and tailored to your business.

1. **Build a Dual-Layered Model**

   Layer 1: Filing Partner (Your Current Consultant)

   - Files returns
   - Maintains documentation
   - Provides routine compliance

   Layer 2: Strategic GST Advisor (Like a Specialist Doctor)

   - Reviews your risk profile monthly
   - Conducts preventive audits
   - Creates SOPs and staff training programs

- Advises on vendor, credit, and structuring
- Handles audits and legal responses end-to-end

2. Ask Better Questions

Stop asking:

"Return file ho gaya na?"

Start asking:

- "What are my top 3 GST risks this month?"
- "Are any of our vendors creating exposure?"
- "Is any ITC at risk of reversal?"
- "Are we due for a preventive GST audit?"
- "Could we reduce liability by changing the billing structure?"

3. Invest in Preventive Reviews

Just like a financial audit or internal controls review, implement a quarterly **GST Health Check**:

- ITC risk scoring
- Red flag identification
- GSTR-2B vs books vs returns audit
- Supplier risk analysis
- SOP gap detection

Bonus Tip

Regularly check for system-generated alerts, scrutiny notices, or risk ratings that hint at upcoming departmental action.

From Reactive to Strategic in 60 Days

A Transformational Real-World Story

A textile trader we worked with (₹80 crore turnover) had:

- Four pending notices
- Two rejected refunds
- ₹14.2 lakhs in disputed ITC

They retained their existing consultant but brought us in as a strategic layer.

Within 60 days:

- The vendor risk system was deployed
- ITC cleanup started
- Standard notice responses and defense packs were created
- Three notices were closed with no demand
- ₹9.5 lakh refund was recovered

The difference wasn't compliance. It was *strategy*.

A Personal Message

Your consultant might be diligent. Honest. Well-meaning. But they're playing the old game, where GST was seen as a routine compliance job.

Today's GST landscape demands more.

It demands legal understanding, forensic thinking, proactive tracking, and strategic structuring. My role isn't to replace your consultant. It's to protect the blind spots they were never trained to see.

Because where routine compliance ends, true protection begins.

CHAPTER 10

THE PEACE OF MIND PLAYBOOK

Your 30-Day Reset from GST Chaos to Control

"I just want to sleep peacefully again."

That's what *Aman (name changed) said when he walked into my office, shoulders heavy with stress and a thick file of GST notices.

- Unfiled clarifications.
- Mismatched returns. ITC reversals.
- Vendor queries.

And a rising fear that one more notice could trigger a full-blown audit.

But four weeks later, Aman was a different man.

- The notices were addressed.
- The mismatches were corrected.
- The mess was mapped, understood, and finally... managed.

What we gave him wasn't just compliance.

- It was clarity.
- It was confidence.
- It was peace of mind.

And this chapter is your blueprint to get there, too.

Whether you're already caught in the tangle of notices or you just want to avoid future disruption, this 30-day plan will reset your GST structure and bring lasting calm.

The 30-Day Peace of Mind Plan

You don't need to fix everything in one day.

You just need to commit one week at a time.

Each layer you add reduces your exposure and restores your control.

Week 1: Clear the Fog

See the reality. No more guessing.

- Pull your GSTR-1, 3B, 2B, and 9 for the past 6–12 months
- Run a basic ITC reconciliation (Books vs GSTR-2B)
- Make a list of your top 20 vendors and check their GSTIN status
- Identify open notices or pending queries and track where they stand
- Compare your GSTR-1 with GSTR-3B (both turnover and tax)
- Cross-check your Trial Balance with the declared GST turnover

What you get:

A clear map of where your GST risks live—no surprises.

Week 2: Clean Up the Core

Stop the bleeding. Fix what's broken.

- Reverse ineligible ITC under Section 17(5)
- Flag vendors with cancelled GSTINs

- Reverse ITC for payments pending beyond 180 days
- Review RCM transactions: pay and claim where missed
- Resolve GSTR-2B mismatches by coordinating with vendors
- Fix any HSN or classification errors in frequently used items

What you get:

A cleaner base. Leakages plugged. Ground regained.

Week 3: Fortify with Systems

Shift from reactive to proactive.

- Set up a monthly GSTR-2B vs Books reconciliation ritual
- Create a Vendor Risk Scorecard to track compliance health
- Build a simple "GST Health Dashboard"
- Appoint a GST SPOC (single point of contact) in your accounts team
- Organize a digital "GST Folder" for each month: invoices, GRs, returns
- Draft simple SOPs for filing, documentation, and notices

What you get:

A structure that keeps your GST hygiene intact, even when people change.

Week 4: Align People and Partners

You can't do this alone, and you shouldn't have to.

- Conduct a 60-minute internal GST training for your finance team
- Educate your top vendors on practices that protect your ITC
- Sit with your consultant—ask the 5 strategic questions:

1. Where are we exposed?
2. What are our recurring ITC red flags?
3. Should we restructure anything for better GST health?
4. If the audit happens tomorrow, are we ready?
5. What's our standard response process?

➢ And if your current setup doesn't offer real advisory, consider bringing in a GST strategy expert

What you get:
A team that thinks before the department does. A circle of support that keeps stress out.

Your Monthly "Peace of Mind" Checklist

Print it. Paste it. Follow it.

This is your GST habit builder:

☑ GSTR-2B vs Book ITC Match

☑ GSTR-1 vs GSTR-3B vs Books Alignment

☑ Vendor GSTIN Status Check

☑ Reversal Tracker (180-day / Blocked ITC)

☑ RCM Pay & Claim Tracker

☑ Notice Log + Response Status

☑ SOP Compliance Review

☑ Communication Log (Vendor & Department)

You didn't start your business to lose sleep over tax letters.

You started it to build something—something valuable, something lasting.

But when GST goes unmanaged, it chips away at that dream, one notice at a time.

That ends now.

Because with the right structure, the right systems, and the right support, GST becomes manageable.

Peace of mind isn't a fantasy. It's a framework. And now you have it in your hands.

A Final Message from the Author

This book was written for the builder. For the creator. For the business owner who didn't get a playbook until now.

You've built your business with courage.

Now protect it with clarity.

If this book gave you even one insight, one relief, one reset, then know this:

You're not alone.

You're not helpless.

And you deserve to grow without fear.

Let's make that your new default.

All the best in your Growth Journey!

Let's Talk Before the Notice Does.

If any part of this book resonated with you, a mismatch, a vendor issue, or just that quiet anxiety before opening the GST portal, then maybe it's time we talk.

In a short, focused 1-to-1 conversation, we can:

- Map your GST exposure
- Identify blind spots in your current setup
- Explore how to make compliance your strategic advantage

No jargon. No obligation. Just clarity.

Book Your 1-to-1 GST Clarity Call or A Webinar

Because prevention is cheaper than penalties, and peace of mind is always worth the first step.

Scan the QR Code below to take the first step toward peace of mind